A WORLD
THROUGH
MY WINDOW

To Susan 7/99
Happy Birthday
Love Mark

A WORLD THROUGH MY WINDOW

Photographs by
RUTH ORKIN

Text assembled by Arno Karlen

Harper & Row, Publishers

New York • Hagerstown • San Francisco • London

To Mimi and Mortimer Levitt

Copyright acknowledgements will be found on page 119.

A WORLD THROUGH MY WINDOW. Photographs copyright © 1978 by Ruth Orkin. Compilation of quotations copyright © 1978 by Karlen Productions, Inc. All other text copyright © 1978 by Ruth Orkin. All rights reserved. Printed in the United States of America. No part of this book may be used or reproduced in any manner whatsoever without written permission except in the case of critical articles and reviews. For information address Harper & Row, Publishers, Inc., 10 East 53rd Street, New York, N.Y. 10022.

FIRST EDITION

Designed by Michael Perpich

Library of Congress Cataloging in Publication Data

Orkin, Ruth.
  A world through my window.

  1. Photography, Artistic. 2. New York (City)—
Description—Views. 3. Orkin, Ruth. I. Karlen, Arno.
TR654.074   779'.9'97471040924   78-2153
ISBN 0-06-013293-0

78 79 80 81 82 10 9 8 7 6 5 4 3 2 1

Contents

Introduction

Back in Los Angeles, my home town, I'd lived, like a lot of people, on the side of a mountain. Then I moved to New York City, and after a little while in a brownstone there, knew that sooner or later I had to get back on a mountain-side again. So in 1955 I found the closest thing, a fifteenth-floor apartment on Central Park West, just opposite the Sheep Meadow, where, it turned out, you can see everything.

I hadn't thought of my view as a subject for photography at the beginning. I had been a photojournalist for a while, then later a filmmaker, never a scenic photographer. But eventually I started taking pictures, not only because it was there but even more because *I* was. All the time. At home with the kids. That's of prime importance when you're shooting scenery—to be there on a twenty-four-hour-a-day basis. It's the reason scenic photographers live in campers right out on the beach or perched on the edge of a canyon—so they can be right there when conditions are right, so they can be there when anything happens.

Housewife, scenic photographer. My situation was ideal, I suppose (although I don't remember thinking of it quite that way at the time). My children, of course, were also there on a twenty-four-hour-a-day basis, so they got photographed too, just like the view. 6:00 A.M.: mist/feedings . . . 2:00 P.M.: view/playpen time . . . 5:00 P.M.: dusk scene/baths . . . 10:00 P.M.: night shot/baby asleep.

Now that I think about it, I don't see how anyone but a housewife could have got all this done. I can imagine how frustrating it might have been had I been a father/photographer on assignment elsewhere, coming home every day to be told by my wife about what a great cloud formation I'd missed, or to hear about what a funny shot I didn't get of Mary standing for the first time.

Taking pictures out a window isn't so very difficult. Nature has done a lot of the work by giving me sun, clouds, trees, grass, wind, rain and snow. Then there have been the buildings all around and people, of course, who have scattered themselves about to give some extra interest.

In retrospect, it seems one of the main things I did was wait. I waited:
for people, horses, bicyclists, dogs and joggers to get to just the right place
for cars to be the right color
for the right float to come by in a parade
for helicopters to take off or to land
for fireworks to go off
for clouds to become the right shape
for clouds to create a shadow or allow a sunlit space
for the Con Edison smokestacks to blow just right
and for other things, such as lightning while I sat there with the rain coming in, on me and on the floor. I've stayed there waiting—sometimes I didn't even know for what—all bundled up in heavy clothing or drenched from the heat.

I find myself continually pulled to my window, even when I'm busy with something else. More than once a puzzled baby was left, mid-diaper, strapped to the changing table, while I cased the horizon for a change in light. Sometimes, even now, I drag myself out of bed at five-thirty in the morning to shoot a sunrise I think I must have sensed in my sleep. Sounds take me to the window too—voices on loudspeakers announcing events in the park, symphony rehearsals, bongo drums, humming generators for movie lights, helicopter motors, thunder, the pelting of hail, the agonized screech of tires whirling on the ice, and the full, utter silence that follows a big snow.

In general, my photographs are satisfying to me when I find that I've captured exactly what attracted me into taking them in the first place—an exciting light, a fine composition, a lovely pattern. It's also fun knowing that I've had the power, through my camera, to stop something long enough in order to see it properly at all. Cloud movements, erratic storms, lightning, all occur so fleetingly that only the photograph holds them still long enough to be savored.

Within the limitations I've set for myself—three basic lenses, no filters, no tricks—I still find the range of what I get from this one view just overwhelming. When people ask, as almost everyone does, whether these pictures are really all taken from one window, I sometimes feel almost as incredulous as they do—that all this could have been seen and recorded from a single vantage place.

RUTH ORKIN

A WORLD
THROUGH
MY WINDOW

Look to this day!
For it is life, the very life of life.
In its brief course lie all the varieties
and realities of your existence;
The bliss of growth;
The glory of action;
The splendor of beauty;
For yesterday is already a dream,
and tomorrow is only a vision;
But today, well lived, makes every yesterday
A dream of happiness, and every tomorrow
a vision of hope.
Look well, therefore, to this day!
Such is the salutation of the dawn

10

RIG VEDA

Park Lights

New York may indeed be jagged in her long leanness where she lies looking at the sky in the manner of some colossal hair-comb turned upward and so deprived of half its teeth that the others, at their uneven intervals, count doubly as sharp spikes. . . . The fatal "tall" pecuniary enterprise rises where it will in the candid glee of new worlds to conquer; the intervals between take whatever foolish little form they like; the sky-line, eternal victim of the artless jumble, submits again to the type of the broken hair-comb turned up.

HENRY JAMES

12

Lavender Haze

My window shows the traveling clouds,
Leaves spent, new seasons, alter'd sky,
The making and the melting crowds:
The whole world passes; I stand by.

GERARD MANLEY HOPKINS

North Woods

Think of the storm roaming the sky uneasily like a dog looking for a place to sleep in, listen to it growling . . .

ELIZABETH BISHOP

16

Rain Cloud

Tree at my window, window tree,
My sash is lowered when night comes on;
But let there never be curtain drawn
Between you and me.

18

ROBERT FROST

My Tree

*The great vision of the city is burning in your heart in all its
enchanted colors just as it did when you were twelve years old and
thought about it. You think that same glorious happiness of
fortune, fame, and triumph will be yours at any minute, that you
are about to take your place among great men and lovely women in
a life more fortunate and happy than any you have ever
known—that it is all here, somehow, waiting for you and only an
inch away if you will touch it, only a word away if you will speak
it, only a wall, a door, a stride from you if you only knew the place
where you may enter.*

20

THOMAS WOLFE

Temple Emanu-El After a Rainstorm

Central Park South

Jogger in the Snow

. . . *the immutably gray sky, the imperial brightness of the buildings, and the eternal snow on the ground.*

RIMBAUD

22

Plaza in the Snow

On one of those nights of frozen silence when the cold is so intense that it numbs one's flesh, and the sky above the city flashes with one deep jewelry of cold stars, the whole city, no matter how ugly its parts may be, becomes a proud, passionate, Northern place: everything about it seems to soar up with an aspirant, vertical, glittering magnificence to meet the stars. One hears the hoarse notes of the great ships in the river, and one remembers suddenly the princely girdle of proud, potent tides that bind the city, and suddenly New York blazes like a magnificent jewel in its fit setting of sea, and earth, and stars.

There is no place like it, no place with an atom of its glory, pride, and exultancy. It lays its hand upon a man's bowels; he grows drunk with ecstasy; he grows young and full of glory, he feels that he can never die.

24

THOMAS WOLFE

Central Park West Snow

He who looks in through an open window never sees as much as he who looks at a window that is shut . . . What we can see in the sunlight is always less interesting than what transpires behind the panes of a window. In that dark or luminous hole, life lives, life dreams, life suffers.

BAUDELAIRE

Central Park South Windows

Car on the Sidewalk

Shriner Parade

Balloonists have an unsurpassed view of the scenery, but there is always the possibility that it may collide with them.

H. L. MENCKEN

Balloon

The city is the place where men are doomed to wandering forever
. . . one yet remembers it as a place of proud and passionate
beauty; . . . the place where men feel their lives will gloriously be
fulfilled and their hunger fed.

THOMAS WOLFE

Low-Hanging Fog

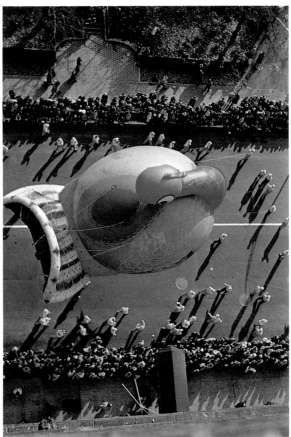

The Turkey

36

Orange Autumn

Even residents who have learned to take New York for granted are,
on occasion, awed . . . by the citadel of riches . . . that is New York.

IRWIN EDMAN

Christmas Tree

The morning, which is the most memorable season of the day, is the awakening hour. Then there is least somnolence in us; and for an hour, at least, some part of us awakes which slumbers all the rest of the day and night. . . . The Vedas say, "All intelligences awake with the morning. Poetry and art, and the fairest and most memorable of the actions of men, date from such an hour. . . . Morning is when I am awake and there is a dawn in me."

HENRY DAVID THOREAU

Winter Sunrise

The eye marveled—marveled at the dazzling whiteness;
The ear hearkened to the stillness of the solemn air;
No sound of wheel rumbling nor of foot falling,
And the busy morning cries came thin and spare.

ROBERT BRIDGES

43

White Trees, Central Park South

. . . at night . . . the streets become rhythmical perspectives of glowing dotted lines, reflections hung upon them in the streets as the wisteria hangs its violet racemes on its trellis. The buildings are a shimmering verticality, a gossamer veil, a festive scene-drop hanging there against the black sky to dazzle, entertain, amaze.

44

5:00 P.M., Winter

Pruning Trees

Kite Day

. . . I perceive the spring in the softened air.

HENRY DAVID THOREAU

all the creatures seemed to enoy the game
in the circus, with their circus people.

D. H. LAWRENCE

Circus Press Conference

Ten thousand vehicles careering through the Park this perfect afternoon. Such a show; and I have seen all—watch'd it narrowly, and at my leisure. Private barouches, cabs, and coupés, some fine horseflesh—lapdogs, footmen, fashions, foreigners, cockades on hats, crests on panels—the full oceanic tide of New York's wealth and "gentility." It was an impressive, rich, interminable circus on a grand scale, full of action and color in the beauty of the day, under the clear sun and moderate breeze.

WALT WHITMAN

Rolls-Royce Luncheon

The people seated on the benches fanned out in front of the band shell are attentive, appreciative. In the trees the night wind stirs, bringing the leaves to life, endowing them with speech; the electric lights illuminate the green branches from the under side, translating them into a new language. Overhead a plane passes dreamily, its running lights winking. On the bench directly in front of me, a boy sits with his arm around his girl; they are proud of each other and are swathed in music.

E. B. WHITE

Philharmonic Concert

Mickey Mouse

*The spectacle of New York remains—infinitely grand and gorgeous.
. . . The town seizes upon all the more facile and agreeable emo-
tions like band music.*

H. L. MENCKEN

Marching Band

The people will live on.
The learning and blundering people will live on. . . .
There are men who can't be bought. . . .
The fireborn are at home in fire. . . .

CARL SANDBURG

Antiwar Lie-In

You woke in the morning
And saw the sky still clouded, the street
*   still wet,*
But nobody noticed so much, except the taxis
And the people on parade

STEPHEN VINCENT BENÉT

Last Big Peace March, 1972

Fireworks

. . . Nature oftentimes breaks forth
In strange eruptions;

SHAKESPEARE

3:00 P.M., The Brown Storm

A hundred times I have thought: New York is a catastrophe, and
fifty times: it is a beautiful catastrophe.

LE CORBUSIER

Blackout, November 9, 1965

Ah filthy New York . . .
What angel do you carry, concealed in your cheek?

F. GARCÍA LORCA

Con Ed Stacks

After the Red Rainbow

Black Clouds Over the Carlyle Hotel

New York had all the iridescence of the beginning of the world.

F. SCOTT FITZGERALD

Mist Over the Sheep Meadow

I am lost in a city, or in Nature? New York is no protection from the violence of Nature. It is a city of open sky. The storms overflow its streets, which are so wide and long to cross when it rains. Blizzards shake the brick houses and sway the skyscrapers. In summer the air trembles between the houses, in winter the city is flooded, so that you might think you were in the suburbs of Paris when the Seine had overflowed, though it is only the snow melting.

JEAN PAUL SARTRE

Lightning Over the Sheep Meadow

Crossing a bare common, in snow puddles, at twilight, under a clouded sky, without having in my thoughts any occurrence of special good fortune, I have enjoyed a perfect exhilaration.

RALPH WALDO EMERSON

Sidewalk Footprints

I see the spectacle of morning . . . from daybreak to sunrise . . .
The long slender bars of clouds float like fishes in the
sea of crimson light.

RALPH WALDO EMERSON

GM Building at Sunrise

The Sherry-Netherland Tower

They did not say,
"This will make life better, this is due to the god,
This will be good to live in." They said "Build!"
And dug steel into the rocks.

They were a race
Most nervous, energetic, swift and wasteful,
And maddened by the dry and beautiful light
Although not knowing their madness.
So they built . . .

STEPHEN VINCENT BENÉT

78

Clear Morning, Central Park South

Our horizon is never quite at our elbows. . . .
My nearest neighbor is a mile distant. . . .

HENRY DAVID THOREAU

Rainbow Over Fifth Avenue

I think this city is full of people wanting inconceivable things.

JOHN DOS PASSOS

Citicorp Pink

Here is the great city, and it is lush and dreamy.
A May or June moon will be hanging like a burnished
silver disc between the high walls aloft.

84

Moonlight #2

Andy and Morris Sledding

Mary Watching the Balloon

Morris Buttering Bread

86

Family Portrait in the Parking Lot

Little Pink Clouds

*At last we were one with New York. . . . I remember riding in a
taxi one afternoon between very tall buildings under a mauve and
rosy sky; I began to bawl because I had everything I wanted and
knew I would never be so happy again.*

F. SCOTT FITZGERALD

PHOTOGRAPHER'S
NOTES

Every picture in this book has been taken from one window on the fifteenth floor at 65 Central Park West, between Sixty-sixth and Sixty-seventh streets, from 1955 to 1978, a period of twenty-three years.

My apartment faces east toward the Fifth Avenue side of Central Park, with the East River and Queens beyond that. To my right and to the south are Central Park South and Midtown Manhattan. To my left and to the north are Harlem and the Bronx. To my back and to the west are Lincoln Center, the Hudson River, and, of course, California. The invariable eastern view means that I can never shoot an actual sunset, only sunrises. All my sunsets here are reflections of the sunset on buildings or on the clouds.

We actually have several windows facing the park, but only the living room has one with no air conditioner that's really convenient. A dining table between the two windows is a handy spot for my cameras and lenses when I'm "on duty." Otherwise one camera is always kept ready and loaded in a cabinet nearby. Summer and winter, I photograph from an open window. I don't shoot through the glass, because that would cut down on sharpness, and also I wouldn't have enough mobility that way. There are bars on the windows, so I'm left with an eleven-inch space in which to maneuver. The bars are there not only because of the children but because New York sills are much too low for leaning out safely.

As for cameras, I started with a Contax, then went to a Nikon F with, essentially, just three lenses: 50 mm, 135 mm and, starting in 1970, a 28-mm Vivitar. Of the 55 photographs in the book, 30 are 50 mm, 19 are 135 mm, 3 are 28 mm. There are also one done with a borrowed 8-mm fisheye, one with a borrowed 500 mm, and one with a 270 mm (with extender).

The film used was always the fastest Kodachrome Kodak was making at the time. Until recently it was KX, now it's Kodachrome 64; all was daylight type, with some early exceptions. For time exposures I use a clamp on the top window bar. A regular tripod is useless, because then the camera ends up inside the room. I have used cable releases, but more often I've just held my finger on the shutter release for seconds, or even minutes. The meters used were, originally, the Weston II, now the Luna Pro. I don't bracket the exposures often, because I tend to trust my meter and don't really want to shoot too many pictures I know will be either over or under.

I don't use filters. If a picture is pink, yellow, blue, brown or lavender, that's because the original scene looked that way. I want people to see what I saw myself, and filters don't help with that. I admit that filters, along with other devices, such as darkroom manipulation, might turn out some striking, even worthwhile, photographs, but they wouldn't be my view.

All of the color pictures here are reproduced full-frame.

Following are my recollections about the shooting of some of the individual pictures in the book.

Page 11. *Park Lights* (1968). This is a morning shot. The lights were all the old-style incandescent ones and they made a lovely pattern in the dawn. Now they're using mercury vapor lamps and I can't get this sort of view anymore.

Page 13. *Lavender Haze* (early 1970s). Another morning shot, the light coming from the left (east). I don't remember seeing anything like this before, and I haven't seen it since.

Page 15. *North Woods* (1960). This view, looking uptown and across the park, happens to be an autumn shot, but what really makes it a photograph is that the skyline is in the shade so that your eye goes to the sky and the trees, not to the buildings. A spectacular day!

Page 17. *Rain Cloud* (1976). I used a lot of film on this spectacular cloud formation. Actually the whole sky was impressive that day, and I did quite a few shots with the wide angle. These didn't work nearly as well, though, the broad sky diluting the dramatic effects of one fine cloud with great billows above and a rainstorm below. A happy element in the picture is that the Fifth Avenue buildings below are barely lit, so that there's no distraction from the main subject.

Page 19. *My Tree.* I've always called this my tree because it's so nicely shaped and in just the right spot to do service in many different kinds of pictures. This was shot in the rain and I was attracted by the people taking shelter there.

Page 21. *Temple Emanu-El After a Rainstorm.* Rain creates a variety of light. Here I had noticed a combination of receding storm clouds . . . the purple sky . . . and the golden glow of a setting sun. Temple Emanu-El is the building with the arched entrance. It's a Fifth Avenue landmark.

Pages 22-23. Snow pictures are the favorites of everyone—including photographers—and there are quite a few of them in this book. There are surely some good reasons for this. First, snow provides good contrast and good backgrounds. In winter, colors are generally fairly dull and most views lack distinctiveness. Snow, however, outlines anything that's dark and shows up details vividly. Second, snow provides striking effects because it acts as a giant reflector, lighting up the whole scene in unusual ways.

Jogger in the Snow (1977). Snow makes the picture. If it weren't for the snow on the ground, the bare branches of the tree would hardly show. But the low sun is a factor here too. Without it, the tracks in the snow wouldn't be seen and the picture would lose a great deal in the way of texture.

Central Park South, 28 mm (1976). A classic snow situation—practically a black-and-white photograph.

Plaza in the Snow (1976). A picture like this requires a number of elements that must mesh just right. There must be a heavy snowfall . . . it must stop during the day . . .

there must be no sun to melt the snow from the trees . . . and it must be a weekend or a holiday so that there will be some people in the park. This particular shot was made on December 26, 1976. A couple of people had come through earlier, but not in the right spot. Fortunately they came through again half an hour later.

Page 25. *Central Park West Snow* (1959). It had been a spectacular snow, followed by one of those sparkling nights that come after the storm blows off. I just leaned way out looking downtown—my own building's façade appears on the right of the picture—and made a good long exposure. As with other night snow shots, you can see the reflector effects lighting up the buildings on Central Park South. This is an older picture, predating the Huntington Hartford Museum down at Columbus Circle.

Page 27. *Central Park South Windows* (1976). It was a good gray day, which helped keep down the contrast of the buildings, made it look as if they had a common façade. The differences between them were subtler than usual. The whole thing reminds me of some of those Italian hill towns, but on a big-city scale.

Page 28. *Car on the Sidewalk* (1975). It was early Sunday morning. No one was hurt, but it was a fairly frightening accident. The driver of the limousine said that his brakes locked and he plowed into one car and started a chain reaction.

Page 29. *Shriner Parade* (1977). It was like a small-town parade, just a few hundred people. They'd congregated and started heading downtown from around Sixty-eighth Street. Apparently one Shriner was overcome and required medical treatment. The other Shriners, and the parade, went on. The composition here was strictly determined by the subject. The blacktop of Central Park West always works nicely with bright colors.

Page 31. *Balloon* They invariably put balloons up early in the morning. Balloons are supposed to be a nonpolluting, noiseless way of travel, but the escaping hot air always makes a tremendous hissing that wakes us up. Unfortunately, the balloons never go anywhere. They're usually inflated as part of some advertising promotion or another, and the people never throw over enough sandbags to really let them take off. I'd love to see one get loose for a change and just float away over the city. One of the pleasures of this picture, I think, is in that possibility.

Page 33. *English Landscape*. This was exciting because it was a relatively rare occurrence—a real English countryside look with a gray sky and the sun breaking through in places to highlight some lovely greens. I had to wait patiently for the proper balance of light and shade on the ground and light and shade in the sky, and I finally got to take only a very few shots.

Page 35. *Low-Hanging Fog.* Everything was softened by the mist and I loved the look of the great bowl full of fog. The cars are a reminder, though, that this is New York City and not a dream scene.

Page 36. *The Turkey* (1950s). For the past twenty-odd years all my Thanksgivings have been accompanied by Macy's great parade. It's a lot of fun and my New York substitute for the Tournament of Roses in Pasadena, which I never get to see anymore. This turkey is one of the great old balloons. Unfortunately they don't use him nowadays. No one ever sees a turkey quite this way—except on the table. It's nice the way the handlers' costumes match the balloon.

Page 37. *Orange Autumn* (1976). What can you say about autumn? It's so brief in the city that some years I'd never get around to shooting a thing. But 1976 was a great year for colors. I decided to shoot it methodically every three or four days. The biggest job was sorting out everything later, because the differences were so subtle. I picked this one because it has an undistracting dull sky but the fall colors aren't impaired. I have another gorgeous shot, with puffy white clouds in a blue sky, but it is just too busy.

Page 39. *Christmas Tree* (1960s). Many people who see this photograph say, "Oh, isn't it wonderful to have this scene outside your window every year." But in fact, the picture never happened before. Most years there wasn't any snow on the ground when the tree was up . . . or the lights weren't on at dusk . . . or it wasn't this clear . . . or I wasn't home.

I remember I was busy serving dinner to some friends when I glanced out and realized that all the elements were finally just right. I got up from the table as if to go back into the kitchen. Instead I dashed for the bedroom (where I normally never shoot), fastened the camera to the window bars, and took a series of various exposures. There was no way of being sure without bracketing. I thought to myself: They're going to feel neglected when they discover where I've disappeared—that I've gone and left them just to take pictures. The picture is one of my most popular, and UNICEF has now used it for several years as one of their Christmas cards.

Page 41. *Winter Sunrise.* The Tavern on the Green's Christmas tree is in this picture, but it's only a minor element. What's important here is the weak sun, the paled-out colors and mostly the chilly dampness. This picture makes me feel as cold as any I've done.

Page 43. *White Trees, Central Park South* (1967). There have been very few days over the years when the snow has clung to the trees as thickly as this. City conditions just don't seem to be right most of the time. It had been one of the winter's heaviest snowfalls. All the cars were thoroughly buried and people walked down the center of the streets. It was incredibly quiet.

Page 45. *5:00 P.M., Winter* (1950s). Another snow picture, but the fact is that if it weren't for the snow, this would be an ordinary postcard shot The snow in the foreground just lights the whole picture up like a huge white reflector. If there'd been no snow, I'd have had to aim the camera higher and concentrate on the sky. The foreground wouldn't have been worth including.

Page 46. *Pruning Trees* (1964). The noise of his electric saw got me to the window. I popped on my 135-mm lens and that was it. The dark-colored cutfit, the orange sawdust, the pale-green trees—that was the picture. Every year until the budget crunch began, you could hear that sound and know spring had come.

Page 47. *Kite Day* (1967). The first Kite Day was held during the sixties. The pattern here could happen only because the Sheep Meadow was cleared of all its usual soccer, baseball and volleyball players and because the kite fliers spaced themselves out so nice and evenly. There were some kites in the air, but more of them were still on the ground at this point, and that's what makes the picture work. Kites in the sky, especially en masse, have never looked good from my view. There's just too little contrast.

Page 49. *Circus Press Conference* (1975). Before 1976, when the Tavern on the Green changed management, the Tavern parking lot was literally a fairground as publicity events were staged, mini-conventions were held, fashion shots were taken, tents were raised for exhibits. Countless new products were photographed there too, including a new bicycle with ten-inch wheels, which I later bought. This photograph was made in spring just after the circus arrived in town. A lot of animals and performers came over to the Tavern to generate publicity and let the press get some shooting in. The only way to understand what's going on is to be above it, as I was. It looked like chaos, but when I could isolate a portion of the scene with my camera, it began to take on order. My favorite part is the two enigmatic red lines which focus your interest and somehow make the scene look as if it has some purpose.

Page 51. *Rolls-Royce Luncheon* (1969). These festivities were held at the Tavern on the Green and seemed to consist mainly of the owners' admiring each other's cars. I had a bird's-eye view and the scene gave me just the right combination of subject, distance and angle. Everything's outlined nicely against the asphalt and the colors are good and soft. It was great fun to watch.

Page 53. *Philharmonic Concert* (1975). No concert I've seen has ever been as crowded as this one. André Kostelanetz was conducting and the people just kept coming and coming. You wondered if they'd ever stop. Afterward we went down and saw that there were thousands more under the trees and stretching out beyond the paths and walks. Probably some of it was the fact that the *1812 Overture* was on the program and there were going to be fireworks after. The dusk shooting was difficult, as the light was continually changing and I constantly had to take new readings.

Page 54.   *Mickey Mouse* (1977). This picture is one of the latest ones in the book, done on Thanksgiving Day during the Macy's parade. The man holding one of the dozens of lines looks here as if he's the only one supporting Mickey, and he's clearly delighted at the sheer fun of it all. He's probably a Macy's employee, as are most of the people in the parade. That Thanksgiving my daughter Mary and I had gone to watch them blow up the balloons around midnight on Seventy-seventh street. A couple of hundred other people also had the same idea. It was a festive but rather deflating sight to see all the balloons stretched out flat on their tummies, reaching from CPW to Columbus Avenue. This shot was tough in that I was dealing with a moving subject, whose appearance constantly changed through the frame of my window. I was pleased to have caught him in just the right position.

Page 55.   *Marching Band* (1977). I was attracted by the white hats and the orderly lines of this band in the Macy's Thanksgiving Day Parade. It's a perfect subject for a straight-down picture.

Page 57.   *Antiwar Lie-In* (1969). These people are demonstrating against the Vietnam war. They lay down on the ground even though it was terribly muddy, all of them holding balloons—white for soldiers who were still alive, black for the dead. Then, on a signal, they all released their balloons at once. This is something I would have shot whether or not it was good photographically, because it's historically important. In fact, though, it's interesting to see people scattered around in unaccustomed poses and to catch the balloons against the sky.

Page 59.   *Last Big Peace March* (1972). The first big Peace March, in March 1967, was enormous, and so was this last one. It rained and it rained, but the people just kept on coming, lots of them with children and babies in strollers. I also shot the march looking up Central Park West so you could see the crowds stretching off into the distance, but this view worked out better. When you look straight down on the umbrellas, the patterns and the colors really are lovely. Also this picture has more intimacy—even from 15 stories up. It's nice to be able to see some faces.

Pages 60-61.   *Fireworks.* Fireworks are all-time favorites—to watch and to photograph. These were taken over a period of years, mostly on New Year's Eve, when they're set off from the Ramble and fall into the rowboat lake. Everyone who's young enough or has good enough circulation stands around Bethesda Fountain to watch. It's great fun in our house, as it's Mary's birthday. The two green shots were made without tripods. I just held open the shutter until the fireworks exposed the film, then closed up.

Page 63.   *3:00 P.M., The Brown Storm* (1969). I thought the world was coming to an end. The rain just looked absolutely crazy. In great gusts it went here and there, in every direction. It was really scary—the movement, the sound, the color; almost complete blackness in a matter of minutes, at three in the afternoon! Another photographer told me he'd been watching it from Riverside Drive, and he thought the whole world had turned green. At any rate, everyone in the city knew it was something monumental. All the newspapers commented on it.

Page 65. *Blackout, November 9, 1965.* This picture was shot by the light of the moon, I think at two to four minutes. Notice the shadows under the trees. I could see them with my bare eyes. They're not normally visible when all the park and building lights are on. Here the lights in the buildings are candles, the lights in the streets are from headlights, and the lights in the sky are from helicopters. Why is the sky green? Because my camera happened to be loaded with daylight-type film.

Page 67. *Con Ed Stacks.* For once, pollution gave me a fine view here. The picture would have been kind of dull with only the buildings silhouetted against the red sky. The black smoke gives it some real composition.

Page 68. *After the Red Rainbow.* This is the way it really looked, believe it or not. It was late afternoon, and two friends were visiting. Suddenly one of us noticed that the light outside had turned a deep rose pink. Running to the window in my workroom, we saw the most incredible sight: a totally pink sky, a totally pink rainbow . . . a totally pink world. Unreal! Fantastic! I only saw it for the blink of an eye because it immediately sent me racing into the living room for my camera. One of the disadvantages of being a photographer is that many times you can't fully appreciate an event while it's occurring, only later as you may remember it. The shot I got of the red rainbow doesn't look very real, but even when the blue started to come back into the sky, and the clouds weren't solid pink anymore, the earth and buildings were still an unearthly color. And this is it.

Page 69. *Black Clouds over the Carlyle Hotel.* The clouds got into just the right position for me— even the swirls were right. This picture was a matter of recognizing a rare set of conditions and *grabbing* the shot. The view looks odd, but the darks were that dark and the lights that light. This was one case where I did bracket to make sure.

Page 71. *Mist over the Sheep Meadow* (1971). You don't see mists in New York as often as in other places, and I'd certainly never seen a mist rolling over the meadow quite this way before. It was 6:00 A.M., and as the sun came up the mist kept moving constantly, looking very white and soft. The silhouetted trees and buildings help make the picture.

Page 73. *Lightning over the Sheep Meadow.* This is a long exposure done without a tripod. The lights in the buildings kept jiggling around because they were the only things being recorded on the film. Then when the lightning struck it gave enough extra illumination for the building outlines to be recorded.

99

Page 75. *Sidewalk Footprints.* It was a warmish day and the snow was fairly wet, which meant that the melted-through places, such as the footprints, made for nice contrast. This close-up, shot right across the street with the 135 mm, picked up a simple composition of the footprints, a bench and the parked VW.

Page 77. *GM Building at Sunrise* (1975). A fine pink sky, some strong city shapes, and a picture.

Page 78. *The Sherry-Netherland Tower* (1976). I'd love to be able to get into a helicopter, buzz around, and shoot head on all the beautiful building tops of Manhattan. I settled here for a close-up with a borrowed 500-mm telephoto. The General Motors Building makes a bland backdrop for the ornate hotel tower.

Page 79. *Clear Morning, Central Park South* (1976). This is the most beautiful time of day for me. It is very, very early, when the morning light is so crisp and clean I can smell the foliage in the park.

Page 81. *Rainbow over Fifth Avenue* (1950s). Rainbows make people feel good, and the nice thing is they're not difficult to shoot. All you need is color film, and then you just point your camera. This is the only classic rainbow I remember shooting, though, because they don't happen often in the city. Actually, it's a double. This is an early shot. Notice the now demolished Savoy Plaza Hotel at the extreme right.

Page 83. *Citicorp Pink* (1978). New York sunsets are often impressive, but this one was as intense a color as I'd encountered in a long time. You can see the red in all the west-facing windows, but what was special was obviously the spectacular reflective power of the new Citicorp building. It's faced with aluminum panels, which just seem to glow when the sun is right.

Page 85. *Moonlight #2.* I call it moonlight, but it wasn't. It was, in fact, a bright sun and I underexposed it a lot.

Pages 86-87. I don't think it should be forgotten that all the pictures in this book were done not just from a window but from the window of the place where I live. My daily round and the daily rounds of my family were part of the story, and when I was shooting "my world" I was as often shooting them as I was photographing strangers or sunsets or skyscrapers. Sometimes I saw my family through the window—or at it—and these are some examples.

Andy and Morris Sledding (1965). I've been fortunate in being able to look out my window and see my children playing in the park—at the sledding hill, the Tavern parking lot, the Sheep Meadow, and in the playground when the trees weren't too thick.

Mary Watching the Balloon (1971). Mary was nine here. We keep two pairs of binoculars in the cabinet along with the cameras.

Morris Buttering Bread. When we first moved here we had the table made to fit between the two windows. This was a stereo camera shot from when I was doing that sort of thing.

Family Portrait in the Parking Lot. Morris Engel, my husband, Andy, age seven, Mary, age four, posing for me on a Sunday morning before baseball practice with a bag full of plastic balls.

Page 89.   *Little Pink Clouds* (1974). It was there and I shot it. I made quite a few exposures. The darkness of the trees in the foreground makes the buildings look as if they're reaching especially high.

ALSO FROM
MY WINDOW

Certainly not everything I see from my window is pretty scenery. The regular round of city life generates a lot of activity that is less picturesque, perhaps, but still worth shooting. Some of this is action photography, and most of it I've shot in black and white because it reflects a photojournalistic vision. A few were done in color, though, and converted from my transparencies. The important thing is that all of this is also a part of the world from my window.

Earth Day, 1971.   People out on the Sheep Meadow started a
bonfire of police barriers to warm themselves against the cold.
Police on horseback and in jeeps chased them in what some ob-
servers called a police riot.

1975.   Crowds leave a symphony concert in the Sheep Meadow.
They lend a party atmosphere to Central Park West and Sixty-
seventh Street as they block traffic.

1977.   A multi-car accident on Central Park West. Several
people were badly injured.

1967. The first and the biggest of the peace marches. People came from all over the country and marched from Central Park to the United Nations.

1967. Also the first big peace march. People waiting to join the line of march are burning their draft cards.

1975. The War Is Over demonstration. A lovely spring day and a grand celebration, with banners and balloons flying, and folk and rock entertainment.

1969. Six thousand people were snowbound at Kennedy Airport for three days following a spectacular blizzard. The police helicopter has just taken off with a load of food for the stranded travelers.

1975.   A guest during a party leaned out and spotted this sign just as the three young teenagers had finished it. It took a lot of yelling to get them to stand still in the freezing temperature for a 4-second exposure. Two of the boys were sons of my friends in the building.

1969.   This geodesic dome was erected in the Tavern on the Green parking lot in the course of one morning.

1963.   The cobblestones in the parking lot and in front of the Tavern on the Green are being covered over by asphalt. Fashion and advertising photographers used to make good use of them for backgrounds.

1968.   The parking lot was also a departure place for children heading off to summer camp. Parents came to see the children off.

1977.   A big warehouse fire, early one Sunday morning, caused this spectacular scene. The fire was to the south and behind me on the Hudson River, but winds had blown the billowing clouds toward the East River.

1966.   A park building just west of the carousel was burning
and making a terrific amount of smoke. It was totally destroyed.

1977.   Many movies are shot in the park. This is Milos Forman's
production of *Hair,* with the dancers cavorting down our favorite
sledding hill.

1978.   The six-mile Mini-Marathon for women, the latest photo in the book, shot June 3, 1978.

Central Park South, 1955.   This shot, a conversion from color, is the oldest I have. The RCA building, 500 Fifth Avenue, the Empire State Building are all now covered up by boxy skyscrapers. The Chrysler Building is almost hidden by 666 Fifth Avenue.

Central Park South. 1978.   The three new structures on CPS are two apartment houses west of Seventh Avenue in the center of the picture and the white marble museum built by Huntington Hartford at Columbus Circle. The Columbus Circle monument can be seen in both the older and the more recent photographs, as can the Paramount Building down near Times Square, which is identified by a little round ball of the world on top.

SOURCES OF QUOTATIONS

PAGE

10   Rig Veda.
12   Henry James. "New York Revisited" in *Travels in America* (1958).
14   Gerard Manley Hopkins. "The Alchemist in the City" (1865).
16   Elizabeth Bishop. "Little Exercise" (1933).
18   Robert Frost. "Tree at My Window" (1916).
20   Thomas Wolfe. *From Death to Morning* (1935).
22   Rimbaud. "The Illuminations."
24   Thomas Wolfe. "Enchanted City" in *The Web and the Rock* (1935).
26   Baudelaire. "Windows."
30   H. L. Mencken. "The Bend in the Tube" in *Prejudices, Sixth Series* (1927).
32   Cyril Connolly. "La Clé des Chants" in *The Unquiet Grave* (1957).
34   Thomas Wolfe. "Enchanted City" in *The Web and the Rock* (1935).
38   Irwin Edman. "The Spirit Has Many Mansions" from the *New York Times* (1953).
40   Henry David Thoreau. *Walden* (1854).
42   Robert Bridges. "London Snow" (1880).
44   Frank Lloyd Wright. *The Disappearing City* (1932).
47   Henry David Thoreau. *Journal* (1858).
48   D. H. Lawrence. "When I Went to the Circus" (1929).
50   Walt Whitman. "May 1879, A Fine Afternoon 4 to 6" in *Specimen Days* (1879).
52   E. B. White. *Here Is New York* (1949).
54   H. L. Mencken. "There Are Parts for All in Totentanz" in *Prejudices, Sixth Series* (1927).
56   Carl Sandburg. "The People Will Live On" in *The People Yes* (1936).
58   Stephen Vincent Benét. "Metropolitan Nightmare" (1936).
62   Shakespeare. *King Henry IV, Part I*, Act 2, Scene 4.
64   Le Corbusier. "The Fairy Catastrophe" in *When the Cathedrals Were White* (1947).
66   F. García Lorca. "Ode to Walt Whitman" in *The Poet in New York* (1955).
70   F. Scott Fitzgerald. "My Lost City" in *The Crack-Up* (1932).
72   Jean Paul Sartre. "Manhattan: Great American Desert" in *Town & Country* (1946).
74   Ralph Waldo Emerson. *Nature* (1836).
76   Ralph Waldo Emerson. *Nature* (1836).
78   Stephen Vincent Benét. "Notes to Be Left in a Cornerstone" (1936).
80   Henry David Thoreau. *Walden* (1854).
82   John Dos Passos. *Manhattan Transfer* (1925).
84   Theodore Dreiser. *The Color of a Great City* (1923).
89   F. Scott Fitzgerald. "My Lost City" in *The Crack-Up* (1932).